*"Fibonacci" By Bob Macko*

*"We are experiencing the greatest moments here on earth where transparency is key now. And we are raising our frequencies through our thoughts and our actions to make a difference for this precious planet and its inhabitants."*

Joanne Koenig-Macko

# SURVIVING
# Earth School
# II

## MASTERING YOUR LIFE:

### *The Ultimate Journey*

## Joanne Koenig-Macko

# Surviving Earth School II

**MASTERING YOUR LIFE: *THE ULTIMATE JOURNEY***

Published by:
Joanne Koenig-Macko, LTD.
Naperville, IL.

Other books by Joanne Koenig-Macko:
*Ohio, You Have Something to Crow About!* (Co-authored with the late Jean Binks-Tolles)
*Surviving Earth School,* How to Learn Life Lessons with Joy, Ease and Humor

Every attempt has been made to properly source all quotes.

ISBN: 978-1-54397-986-2

Spirituality/Personal Growth/Healing/Angels/Energy Healing

Library of Congress

Printed in the United States of America
First Edition

## DEDICATION

To my amazing family for all their love and support over the years. I love you more than you'll ever know. Thank you for believing in me and supporting my vision.

To my husband, John, for having patience with me for over 40 years. You are my rock, Saint John.

To my amazing sons, Chris and Bob. I am so proud of you both for the awesome men you've turned into. I encourage you both to follow your passions forever.

To my parents, siblings and ancestors for giving me the DNA that had the dose of courage and fortitude to get this second book done.

To my amazing, precious grandchildren, Luciana Rose, *The Boss*, for your sheer determination and leadership. You inspire me! To my precious Sofia, *The Queen of Hearts*, for your gift of laughter and sensitivity. To William (Will) John, *The Snuggle Master*, for teaching me to constantly learn new things and to make me realize what is truly important in life.

To my beautiful daughters-in-law, Christene and Jane. If I searched the world, I couldn't find better partners for my sons. I love you both so much! Thank you for the gift of my grandchildren and for adding so much joy to our family.

To the special souls in the world for standing in line to be here now! Never quit. The world needs you. Whatever you do in life, make it count.

# ACKNOWLEDGMENTS

Thank you, Bob Macko, for another outstanding cover design.  www.lux-productions.com

Thank you, John Macko, my wonderful husband for teaching me new skills in MS Word and for all the dinners, and edits so I could finally get this book done.

Thank you, Philomena Dias, my kindred spirit soul sister in Australia for encouraging me every step of the way through countless manuscript changes, edits, endless formatting and getting me to the finish line.

Thank you, Laura Michaels for help with editing, even in the wee hours.  I will never put another comma before the word *and*! If I do, I know your eagle eye will catch it.

Thank you to my special Sis, Joyce Grau, my cheerleader and my brother, Bill, for reminding me to just be me.

Thank you to my family and friends on the other side of the veil. I feel your presence always. Love never dies.

Thank you, angels, for keeping me on track even through the storms.

Thank you, John Novak. The other "Lefty" who planted the seed of my curiosity in grade school, 65 years ago.

Thank you, cardinal, for showing up whenever I write.

Ok, Creator, I got the next book done as promised! Thank you for being patient. More to come!

# Contents

# PREFACE

Wow! You liked my first "Surviving Earth School" book and now you're ready to be taken to the next level of your growth, the Master level! See? You followed your lessons, you did your homework and hopefully, you are no longer resorting to throwing

your body against the wall in your rubber room when things don't go your way. Nice work! You've come a long way, kiddo. I'm really proud of you. What's that? You're not even blaming God? Now I'm *really* impressed!

Hey, you have to admit, life sure goes easier when you don't throw tantrums and blame everyone around you for your misfortunes. Well, you can. You know you still have free will and choice because you're just so damn powerful. But what's the point? So hopefully, I gave you a new lens to look at life with. You're always going to be faced with new lessons but now you've got some pretty cool tools from the first book to help you get through life's hiccups.

I've also added lessons and affirmations at the end of each chapter related to what I just wrote and quotes to inspire you, all with a dash of humor. We can all agree that the world needs more positivity and laughter.

Now you realize that YOU create lessons always for your growth and that the turkey who kept poking you in the eye with that stick was your greatest teacher. Thank him or her silently from afar. All they were doing was prodding you and annoying the living daylight out of you so that you could just dig deeper and deeper to see the real belief or beliefs you needed to clear, probably something left over from the Stone Age. When you finally get the lesson, it's the best feeling, isn't it? Woohoo! No one can ever bust your chops again because YOU are then in charge of your own destiny. Now THAT'S true empowerment! You are then unstoppable and the only one in the way is YOU and your crazy little mixed-up beliefs or B.S. that you now realize can be wiped out and replaced with positive affirmations.

I just wish I knew this when I was a lot younger. It would have saved me years of crying on many shoulders, playing the ol' victim, victim game. No one wants to be a member of the BMW club (Bitchers, Moaners and Whiners). So, now that you have some *new* tools to work with. You can put your Superman or Wonder Woman cape on, put your winged warrior sparkle shoes on and soar to the next important level of your life's journey so that you truly make it count! Truth is, you were never broken.

You've learned by now, there's no need to repeat kindergarten here in Earth School unless you really enjoyed playing with the mud pies and stringing those big ol' wooden beads. Hey, some do, so have at it! I'd rather go on to the next level because this is where the real fun starts!

You get to affect others around you! That's where you start making an impact on others. Hopefully, a good one. Once you attain self-mastery, you'll soon realize it's not about you anymore, rather how you can affect others by helping them in some way. Yes, even if you get others to see life in a positive, different way that counts.

Yes, of course you'll still have life lessons but something really powerful happens when the Universe knows that you now know how to see life differently. The cool thing is, you will fly though your lessons so much faster! At the speed of thought! You no longer need to hold onto grudges for months or years. What a brain drain that is. You now see the blessings in what you went through without the martyrdom and you focus on the blessings instead of the burdens. It's like a big weight is lifted off your shoulders. And if you're getting spasms in your shoulders, just know that subconsciously, you're carrying a big load or responsibility you're not dealing with. How can you streamline your life more?

Life actually gets to be fun again! There's a side of you that blossoms and you work from your gifts instead of your traps. You laugh more and create more of what you truly desire and then when that happens, everyone wants to be in your energy field because you're a winner not a whiner! A true survivor! Remember what I taught in the first book, you're a product of the closest five people around you. If you are now a leader because of the transformational work you did, then things fall into place faster and who wouldn't want to be around that awesome energy? It's contagious! Everyone wants to be around a rock star. Even your intuitive levels increase. You're more aware. You have pep to your step! You walk to the beat of a different drummer, not following another guru but leading as a way shower. Nice work!

Enjoy your next evolutionary journey through this book. You've peeled countless layers off already, you're standing taller, straighter and with purpose. You know who you are, what you are, and what makes your heart expand with pure joy. You've learned that competition usually starts its journey in kindergarten. What? Someone's better than you? But your mom said *you're* the best! How can that be? So, you strive to do better, greater and faster! Find the blessing in it. Your competition made you go the extra mile.

You've even learned about the chemical changes in your body when you do kind acts not expecting anything in return. If you do expect something in return, that's simply your ego speaking. Rise above it. Do something to help another, expecting no reciprocation. When you get there, you will be a true master. If you put a condition on something you gave, lent or even bribed, was that from the heart?

Are you ready for your next level? Roll up your shirt sleeves, sharpen your pencils and get on with creating an amazing life!

*Joanne: "Hey Johnny, you like my Mona Lisa?" Johnny: "Hey, Joanne, you like my Eiffel Tower Oatmeal box?"*

"When I was 5 years old,
my mother always told me that happiness was the key to
life. When I went to school, they asked me what I wanted
to be when I grew up.
I wrote down, "happy."

They told me I didn't understand the assignment. I told
them they didn't understand Life."

*John Lennon*

*"Pumpkin Fairy Village" By Joanne Koenig-Macko*

# CHAPTER 1

**ALL TIED UP AND NOWHERE TO GO**

Looking back now over my life, we really do learn so much about life in kindergarten. Think about it. For many of us, it's the first time we're put in a structured situation where we have to learn to share our toys and treat others with respect and to realize there are boundaries.

Some say our personalities are created in the first five years of our lives. That's why I feel it's so important to cover this chapter so that you can review your life to see what stood out in your first five years, usually in kindergarten that could possibly affect you the rest of your life.

We can't just go up to a five-year-old classmate and take their toy just because we want it. Although, I do know a lot of adults today that have no boundaries and wouldn't think twice about stealing ideas, copywritten or not, just because they feel entitled. Ok, for them, there's a special place waiting in Karma Kiddie College, lol.

How did you adjust in those first years of school? That's where your character starts getting defined. It's where your social mores are cast and for many of you, it's a tough ordeal peeling away from your mom's or dad's wall of protection. You're on your own now to fight for the right to that tub of clay or to defend and protect your favorite purple finger paint. Who'll beat you to the easel on Monday morning or to your favorite doll or truck sitting on the shelf? How did you react when one of the kids in kindergarten punched you in the arm with no one to witness it? Did you deal with it? Punch him back? Tattle tale on him to the teacher or go off to cry and hold in your anger until you got home to deck your baby brother in the head with wooden blocks just to get your aggravation out?

Those tender years in school are also reflective on how you deal with situations today. I remember my kindergarten teacher; Miss Sally Siegel She resembled a seagull with her beady little eyes that gave you the glare if you didn't pick up your toys in time for your afternoon nap. She had zero tolerance for the kiddies and I often wondered why the heck she even signed up for that gig.

She could soar over the room, find who was weak, pick them up with her claws and belittle them without a second thought but not before pecking away at their self-esteem with her frosty little beak. She had the empathy of a wet bag of laundry and had no qualms about keeping a child back a year if they didn't pass her ultimate final test of tying a shoelace on this big red, wooden clown shoe. It was ridiculous.

Imagine watching your whole class move forward and you had to stay behind because you couldn't tie Bozo's shoelace. Right there, issues of, "I'm not good enough, I can't keep up," and "Friends abandon me," are set into the subconsciousness to wreak havoc with you as you get into adulthood. Thank God I learned how to tie a shoelace although I know of others who were kept back for that one insane reason. Little did we know Velcro would come along in the future and if we had known about it in the fifties, our classmates would have gladly velcroed Miss Siegel to the blackboard to give her a taste of her own medicine. I'm sure she would have loved a clay facial while we were at it. They say it's great for tightening pores.

Something very valuable is also taught in kindergarten and that's a sense of creating community. If we saw that a child was crying all day because he or she missed his mommy or daddy, we knew how to invite them into our circle of safety and let them know that they were OK. Does that happen today? I don't know, as my grandchildren are just at the age where they're going into that type of environment of preschool. Preschool? We didn't have that in the fifties. Preschool was playing in your backyard with other kids that were too young for school.

Today, the cost to put a child in preschool is equal to a house payment and what you get in return is a carrier of every known disease where the kids should be decontaminated and sprayed with Lysol upon returning home. Hint, buy stock in Kleenex and Boogie Wipes. You'll need it because schools today, especially in major cities are like sending your kid off to the United Nations where every country represented showcases their own unique plague.

Kids know what they want. They must have the latest Shimmer and Shine crystal-laden shoes, dolls that come in a plastic ball with microscopic parts that are smaller than a gummy bear. You'll have to figure out how to get a

3

plastic molded dress half the size of your pinky onto the pre-shrunk miniature doll, complete with instructions in ten languages. Whoever invented those things should be run off of the planet. Just the shoes alone are half the size of a No. 2 pencil eraser. I'm sure the designer was from another planet of miniature aliens who just wanted to torment the average earthbound parent or grandparent. And don't even think of dressing your daughters or granddaughters unless their shoes give off high-powered light strobes enough to blind you in the dark. The retina-burning electric lights at the base of their shoes blind you like a deer in headlights and radiate enough light just to take your mind off the fact that they are carrying an encyclopedia of contagious bacteria from the preschools that even a bucket full of Elsa gummy vitamins can't even come close to fending off. As my son, Christopher said, "Who knew you could entirely ruin a kid's day by choosing the wrong top to wear."

We still took naps in the fifties or else. Thinking back, our moms were absolutely exhausted after doing endless, back-breaking house chores with no modern conveniences. They had to wash dishes by hand, put the clothes through the wringer or mangle, walk to the bus stops and then walk many blocks to the local grocers dragging a stainless-steel wheelie cart behind them.

I remember walking with my mom to the local grocers in the winter and she'd end up pulling a 20-pound turkey with other grocery items in this wire cart on wheels through wind, sleet, snow or hail. How she dragged that heavy load on a rolling cage through two feet of slush and snow was beyond me. She was fearless.

Our nap time was the only time our moms could get anything done, especially to hang the laundry on lines in the backyard or to smoke a Camel. No, not the animal, silly, Camel cigarettes. Lucky Strikes was another popular brand and don't forget that rugged cowboy touting his pack of Marlboros. He was the picture of health as he rode off into the sunset wielding his branding iron in his leather- gloved hand with a piece of hay placed neatly between his pearly whites.

While the kiddies were getting off on Captain Penny and Mr. Green Jeans, the moms were fantasizing about how the Marlboro Man would carry them off on his trusty steed. To get ready for the Marlboro Man, they'd work out, hoisting a broomstick over their heads to Jack LaLanne in front of their brand new black and white Motorola television sets. What a sight for a little kid to walk into.

The first time I saw my mom working out with a broom, I thought she had lost it. But think about it, they had to be in top shape to hoist those eight-foot long wooden laundry props in the backyard. Wet laundry weighed a ton, carrying it up from the basement. We would run through the sheets and I remember how great they smelled after drying out in the backyard all day, despite the heavy cloud of iron ore and smog in the air from the nearby steel mills.

Back then, any news you needed to know was not done by texting. Neighbors yelled over their fences and sometimes three fences. My mom, Rose aka "Lungs" would scream our names from the back porch and we'd hear her bellow from blocks away to get home for dinner *or else*! How we survived without cell phones is truly a mystery.

Seriously, how did we do it?  We just knew that when the street lights came on, you had to be home, or else!  It was a given, or as Mom would say, "No Ifs, Ands, or Buts!"

What were some of the momisms you remember growing up and how did it affect you today? Do you ever catch yourself using some of your parent's unforgettable phrases that kept you in check?

"Just wait till your father gets home!"

"Cross that bridge when you come to it."

"This too shall pass."

"Stop crying or I'll give you something to cry about!"

"Bored? When I was your age, we played kick the can down the street."

"You can stand on your pointy head all day; you are *not* getting that."

"Quit your caterwauling!"

"Money doesn't grow on trees."

"Who do you think I am? Rockefeller's daughter?"

"You'll shoot your eye out with that!"

"Close the door! Were you raised in a barn?

"You made your bed, now lay in it."

"Who do you think you are? Queen of Sheba?"

"When I was your age, I walked five miles to school."

"No one will marry you if you don't make your sacraments." (I protested going to catechism class.)

"Stay away from dragonflies, they'll sew your ears shut."

"Don't eat watermelon seeds, they'll grow inside you."

"Clean your plate, there are kids starving in China."

"Did you spill salt? Quick! Throw a pinch over your left shoulder."

"Break a mirror and you'll have seven years back luck."

"Step on a crack and break your mother's back."

Your palm would itch? Someone was talking about you or you'll come into money. You didn't marry by the age of twenty-one? Sorry, you were considered an old maid. Seriously? I was late twenty minutes for my own wedding at age thirty-one. I waited until the last tick of my biological time clock before saying "I Do."

I've always had the passion to get to the bottom of so many crazy myths in order to debunk them. What better research to do on the whole "throwing salt behind your left shoulder if you knock the salt shaker over." Remember when I said that most of our silly beliefs are just crazy sayings handed down through generations based on fear? Are you ready to see just how far back this particular old wives' tale goes and how it's engrained in our cellular memory? It dates back to biblical times! The ancients believed that our left side was our bad or sinister side so that if you knocked a salt shaker over, you had to immediately toss the salt over your left shoulder to blind the devil who was behind you.

This all stemmed from, according to biblical lore, Lott's wife looked back on Sodom, the great place of sin. As she did, she turned into a pillar of salt which to them meant the devil was behind her. I've even heard from scholars that in the famous painting, *The Last Supper*, Judas is in the process of knocking over the salt shaker which represents his coming betrayal of Jesus. So there! Proof that we carry on old folk superstitions and just how far back they can be traced. It's crazy. Talk about cellular memory!

Ok, I'm sure there were more but you get the idea. And don't tell me you go under a ladder on the street even to this day! Where did they come up with these mind-boggling expressions? And what's worse, I caught myself repeating some of these doozies raising *my* own kids. Again, a perfect example of just how your parent, their parents and your ancestors' beliefs have an impact on you.

So much of the knowledge handed down to us has been twisted and the information no longer holds true. Beliefs play a huge part of who you are today. That's the only reason I'm bringing these facts up. For the most part, your fears are based on absolute B.S., -- belief systems. I prefer to say bullshit but my deceased mom would probably sneak up on me and backhand me.

We forgot how to think on our own. Everything we were taught about anything has been misconstrued because we didn't have the modern technology, we have today to do further research. You were considered cool if you could afford the complete set of Funk and Wagnalls Encyclopedia. Without it, you caught a bus cross town to the Fleet Avenue library for research. Sixty years later, "Hey Google, where'd I leave my glasses?" Google: "Sorry, I don't understand." Geesh...what good are you?

We were also raised not to question authority. Just like so many cultures in the world, we depended on wisdom handed down by the spoken or written word. How could that knowledge not be altered as it was passed from one generation to another?

To this day, I have to catch myself from throwing salt over my shoulder if I accidently knock the damn shaker over. It's crazy to think what we grew up with that was probably handed down through our lineage. My grandmother, who died before I was born, thought her gift of intuition was a curse from the gypsies.

How else were we mesmerized or brain washed by ancient folk tales or influenced by what we saw on television? Looking back to the good old days, my mom's treat was to get us kids off to the local Harvard Elementary school, yes, I'm a Harvard graduate, so she could watch "Guiding Light" and "As the World Turns." Women had no problem smoking several packs a day while they were pregnant. They were completely hypnotized while getting sucked into the latest new television soap opera and learning about the latest products by Proctor and Gamble that promised to change their lives forever, hence the name *soap operas*. Some of the favorite products at that time were Oxidal, Ivory, and Fels-Naptha. Let's not forget Lava soap, because cleaning the dirt off your hands wasn't good enough, it had to remove the second layer of your skin with enough volcanic grit to eradicate your fingerprints.

The ads in the newspapers were intense as well for these gems. Lux soap had a commercial showing a bar chart proving how women over the age of twenty-five had a much harder chance of landing a man, so you had better use their soap to keep your underarms of your garments fresh! Nothing sells like the fear of body odor, right? Or a man hiding in the bushes with his son telling his little boy that "mommy was on the warpath from doing housework all day" and explained to him that "the best way for her to relax was to take a bath in Ivory soap." Priceless.

After all, cleanliness was next to Godliness back then. Perhaps you had your mouth washed out with Ivory soap for swearing. Thank God, we never had to go through that. I was too afraid of my mom's wrath for even *thinking* a bad word. That woman could wield a stainless pancake flipper better than a Samurai swordsman in the middle of a Mongolian takeover. That was her preferred weapon of choice. Hell, even Mrs. Butterworth was afraid of her.

Talk about keeping things clean, what about our sofas hermetically sealed in clear plastic? You had to figure out how to slowly peel yourself off of them in the summer or conversely, how to stay ON them in the winter without sliding off. Mom went for the Hollywood glam look, bright coral with silver threads and blonde legs. Too bad we weren't allowed on it. She had booby traps and land mines around it so we could only look. Hey, if I'm wearing shorts, I don't want to sit on it anyway. I may be stuck to it forever. Just sayin'. Everything was Saran-wrapped in those days.

I remember one day, while my mom was grocery shopping up the street at the local Pick n Pay, my brother and I were playing in the living room and for some dumb reason we decided to start spinning ourselves into this ten-foot wall of white damask drapery that my mom took great pride in installing. We looked like we were butterflies trapped in white silk cocoons and if we would have kept spinning inside them, the whole ten-foot curtain rod would have come crashing violently down on us.

Our luck, mom walked in the door, trusty grocery cart in tow, just in time to see us completely twisted up in the drapes where you couldn't even see us. Instantly, she grabbed her weapon of choice, the infamous pancake turner and proceeded to smack the hell out of us. We were trapped like rats with nowhere to run and nowhere to hide. I think Martha and the Vandellas later made a song about that. I guarantee you, we stayed away from those drapes after that. To this day, I dislike drapes.

Today's kids are just too busy on their laptops and cell phones to be twisting in drapes for fun anyway. They're too busy learning multiple languages, how to build the next skyscraper and how to invest in their first portfolios for their future corporations. Jesus, I feel like a Neanderthal compared to what the kids are learning and doing today.

11

Just the other day, I was watching my three-year-old grandchild, Will. He gave me detailed information on all the planets and what makes them so unique. He added, "Oh! and Grandma Macko, Pluto is no longer a planet because it's too small! And he went on to shape an "o" with his tiny little fingers to show me that Pluto was the size of a cheerio so therefore it had no life on it. He counted his numbers with ease and spouted off the properties of every planet, including which one was furthest from Earth.

Three years old! I tell you, it's a different world. And to think my kindergarten final was to be able to tie a damn clown shoe in order to advance to first fricken grade. We're in a different era now and we know that the human brain is one of the biggest mysteries. We use a very, very small portion of it, so sky's the limit with these kids today. They're pushing past boundaries and are coloring outside the lines now. My five-year-old granddaughter, Luciana is counting to one-hundred and teaching me the colors in Spanish while my other granddaughter, Sofia, at four, is belting out at the top of her lungs, "This Girl is on Fire!"

**LESSON:**

*Kindergarten and grade school are important steps in life. What memories can you recall from those early developmental stages of your youth that have been set in stone and now control who you are today and how you operate? If you were held behind, what emotions did that evoke and how did it affect your behavior today as an adult?*

*If you cried because you weren't accepted by the friends you wanted, how did that make you feel? Abandonment issues usually start at quite an early age. Some say that even when you were a baby and your mom let you cry yourself to sleep in a dark room, you may be dealing with issues of abandonment now as an adult. It can be terrifying for a one or two-year-old. Issues of "no one hears me" pop up later in life and they tend to speak loudly over others just to be heard.*

*Or maybe you had an imaginary friend but your mom told you were just making that up. It could have been your angel or a deceased loved one but with enough put downs, you learned to shut it off. And if you want to know any facts or details about Planet Neptune, just ask a three-year-old.*

**"Has anyone ever abandoned you?  They have given you the opportunity to move forward with the life you truly deserve so that you could find those who support you.**

**Everything in life is happening for your growth.**

**Perhaps your path has been cleared so that something beautiful and amazing can happen to take you to the next level of your wondrous journey."**

*Joanne Koenig-Macko*

## AFFIRMATIONS FOR CHAPTER 1

I am loved and accepted.

I know my self-worth at all times.

I know how to listen to my natural instincts and my God-given ability of intuition because I was placed on this planet for an amazing purpose.

As a powerful being on this planet, I know that if friends I thought were meant to be with me forever leave, then the Universe is simply making room for more powerful and meaningful relationships to step in for the next level of my awesome growth.

*I am strong enough to know that if I spill salt on the table, I won't die.

I am one with the pancake turner and the drapes shall protect me.

*Damn it, then why do I keep tossing that stuff over my left shoulder?

*Through the eyes of an angel, our precious Sofia.*

# NOTHING TO IT!

Behavior patterns, it appears,

Are formed in very early years...

So, Dad and Mother, keep in mind

As twigs are bent are trees inclined.

Be pliable, but don't be lax.

Control them, but get off their backs.

Know where they are and what they do,

Encourage independence, too.

Although they need to feel secure,

Their lives should never be TOO sure.

Affection's very fine, as such,

But not the kind that clings too much.

And self-expression's also fine

As long as it is kept in line.

"Delinquent parents" must be fools;

It's simple when you know the rules.

**Janet Henry**

# CHAPTER 2

## SEAGULLS AND FIGGY NEWTON

As we climbed up the social and educational ladder from nursery to kindergarten to the early learning years, we soon found out there were consequences if we didn't follow the rules. I find it amazing how a kindergartner can get away with a lot because the mother is usually sad to see her baby go off to  school and she's more than forgiving when little Tommy takes a magic marker to the walls or cuts his sister's ponytail off. They soon learn they can wrap their little chubby fingers around mom and get away with murder.

You go into shock missing that sweet little rug rat who was always around the house to trip over because now he or she is being raised by a total stranger who is with them all day while you're at work trying to pay a mortgage on their dollhouse or toy car collection. Many moms just feel they are no longer needed. It can be depressing for many.

So, look back on your childhood and try to remember if there were any incidents that threw you for a loop and affected you as an adult. Maybe the teacher belittled you in front of the class or maybe as my one teacher at Harvard Elementary School had what she called a "dunce row" so if you got a "D" on your math paper, you were sent to sit in that row of shame where everyone knew you weren't the sharpest tool in the shed. It was humiliating.

That's another teacher we could have done away with, our math and writing teacher, Miss Newman, or "Figgy" Newton as we called her. Her face was a wrinkled prune, with a shock of silver-grey hair. She always wore a coal black dress to school every day and she'd write so hard on the blackboard that the back of her arms would swing wildly enough to create a breeze that sent our papers flying off the desks to the back of the room.

She *never* cracked a smile or her face would have shattered. God forbid, she always had a mean scowl. We were terrified of her when she walked into that room. Oh, my, God, when she corrected your math paper, she marked the paper so hard with her pencil that she always ripped your paper in the process. How many times I saw that terrifying grade of "D" being ripped into my math paper, so hard that it felt like it was being carved not only in my wooden desk top but into my very soul.

One of the most ridiculous things we ever had to do in grade school was to have regular drills in case of a nuclear attack. We'd have to get on the floor, squat and put our hands on top of our heads to prevent nuclear fallout from getting on us. You've got to be kidding! Let me tell you, if a nuclear bomb hit, you wouldn't have to worry about the school standing, let alone your city surviving a blast of that magnitude. But then this was the generation raised on cigarettes and scrubbing floors in a freshly starched apron and six-inch high heels. At least that's how the ads portrayed women. Can you imagine today's mom with even two kids wearing Louboutin's and pulling a twenty-pound

Norman Rockwell turkey out of the oven with a smoking cigarette dangling out of her mouth, while texting how to make a five-star gravy?  Ha! Yeah, not happening. As my five-year-old granddaughter, Luci would say, "Not my style."

Our elementary teachers were big on recycling at Harvard Elementary School where I attended. So, that's another thing we learned from the fifties. Miss Clark always had us bringing in Quaker Oats boxes so that we could create something pretty cool with them.  Of course, our parents didn't appreciate us kids dumping all the oats out on the floor for the sake of making a wishing well, drum or birdhouse that would never be used or disintegrate in the first rain storm. We used the oats boxes for everything from holding our valentine cards to storing birdfeed.

The recycling bug must have bit because my dad used to take the Beechnut baby food glass jars to keep all his small nails, screws and lug nuts in. Remember the paper drives at your elementary school? We'd bring stacks and stacks of used newspapers bundled in twine and pile them against the outside walls of the school, all to recycle yesterday's news and get a few dollars for each classroom.

I'm convince that the paper drives were a lesson in littering. I remember papers flying all over that school yard.

Yep, just throw the papers against the wall, someone else will pick it up. And I remember after we scrubbed Mom's kitchen floor, we'd have to cover the linoleum kitchen floor with newspaper to avoid getting the floor dirty. What the hell?  I'd have to read the cartoons walking to my bedroom by looking down. Here's your sign!

And for many children born to parents from the Great Depression, you had to save *everything.* Thank God my parents weren't hoarders but just watching some of the shows today is enough to make you flip. Who needs 10,000 corks, even if they're dried out and useless? "Oh, we'll find a use for them," they would chant. Like what? Building a new floating coffee table out of them? I don't get it. All you have to do is watch the popular TV show, *Hoarders* to see what people refuse to toss because there *must be a use for it.*

LESSON:

*Recycling is great but you don't need more than five of anything unless it's dinner and silverware. You don't need five hammers, ten screwdrivers, and four sets of suitcases. The more junk you hang onto is simply a security issue with you for fear of someone taking something from you. It's a control issue to boot.*

*Remember, you can't take it with you and you only leave a big mess for your kids to clean up once you're gone. Buy a book on Feng Shui to see how energy moves and how it can be blocked if you have piles of clothes on the floor. For every new item you buy, get rid of something. Goodwill is great and someone else less fortunate can use your size seven dresses from high school.*

*Big disco-honker platform shoes will never return or at least I pray they don't. Men looked ridiculous in high heels not to mention enough gold chains around their necks to make even Mel Fisher jealous. I wonder how many women twisted their ankles when dancing to Donna Summer or the Bee Gees? Fast forward, the disco kings from back then, if still alive, are probably all walking around hunched over permanently from the weight of all that heavy metal they hung off their vertebrae. And, don't even get me started on the silk shirts that were unbuttoned to the waist. I never knew if I should call animal control league, gift them with a wax job or just run like hell.*

"Never let another steal your thunder. Actually, they can't. It's your choice to stoop down to their level if they try to belittle you. There will always be people who do not want you to rise above them and they'll do whatever they can to grab you by the ankle and pull you off the ladder of success. No matter how high the mountain, keep climbing and don't look back."

*Joanne Koenig Macko*

## AFFIRMATIONS FOR CHAPTER 2

I sparkle and shine on my own without the disco ball and take nothing personally.

If someone is meant to be in my life, they will be. I bless them and see the gifts they were to me when they graced my life with their presence.

I am powerful enough to stand in my own giftedness.

When I radiate my inner light, I attract like or higher vibration to me.

I know how to allow my children their own space to grow into amazing game changers on this planet. I am beyond blessed to be able to watch them grow into their true magnificence.

Just a tip, even Good Will won't accept disco clothes and platform shoes from the seventies. Burn 'em or have a Disco Inferno party. It's time. The Bee Gees would be proud of you.

I recently came across a book of poetry that is falling apart at the seams. It was my mom's favorite book. I opened it up to find a dried rose and this poem happened to be on that same page:

## INSPIRATION

You never can tell when you do an act
Just what the result will be,
But with every deed you are sowing a seed,
Though the harvest you may not see.
In God's productive soil;
You may not know, but the tree shall grow
With shelter for those who toil.

You never can tell what your thoughts will do
In bringing you hate or love,
For thoughts are things and their airy wings
Are swifter than carrier doves.
They follow the law of the universe –
Each thing must create its kind,
And they speed o'er the track to bring you back
Whatever went out from your mind.

*Ella Wheeler Wilcox*
**From: *The Best Loved Poems***
***of the American People, 1936***

## JUST BEGINNING

"When you reach the age of seventy, you may feel you're growing old but believe me when I tell you, the best years now unfold. Each day has mellow meaning and you have that tender touch from each moment you take gladness, for the years have taught you much. Little things become important. You are prone to find the good. And the things you took for granted are more clearly understood.

True, you cannot run as you did but each step you take is art, for it has been truly written blessed are the young at heart. Life is beautiful in summer, still the autumn has its bliss and you capture more completely memory's enchanting kiss. So, it is when you reach old age, faith is strong and smiles are winning.

Your life is far from over, in fact it's just beginning."

*Anonymous*

# CHAPTER 3

**WHEN DO WE REALLY GRADUATE?**

Good question! For some, they graduate when they actually get a piece of parchment proving they paid their private school or college countless thousands of dollars. Instead of calling it a diploma, I say it should be called a "receipt." That's what it is. There is no guarantee you'll get a job once you pay for all those classes on how  to dissect a frog or recite Shakespeare. The purpose of this chapter is for you to reflect on your past experiences to see how they shaped who you are today. If you were a shy wallflower, what happened in life to snap you out of that syndrome?

What cracks me up are the professors teaching business classes. Most of these people have never stepped a foot into the modern working office...ever. So, no one comes out with any true idea on what it's like in the REAL world. The average student graduates college with $100,000 in debt and the government, bless their hearts, will not forgive those debts. I've seen friends with Ph.D.'s managing 711 stores. And, most do not know how to balance a checkbook once they do step into the real world.

They charge everything, even a Starbuck's latte on a daily basis and then wonder how they ended up with $40,000 in credit card debt. We've become a plastic society.

There are simply no classes to take on how to deal with these real-life problems. Instead, they should teach courses on how to deal with sexual harassment at the work place or how to deal with the gossip mongers at the water cooler or in my case when I worked in the corporate world in the seventies and eighties, one of my co-workers was a Jehovah's Witness. Every morning as I was busy at my desk, he'd stand over my typewriter and tell me how to get to the Kingdom whether I wanted to go or not. Hey, if it wasn't the Magic Kingdom in Orlando, I wasn't interested. I put up with a lot back then while working for various ad agencies.

Every president of every ad agency had a full liquor locker stocked with more booze than you could shake your fist at. Just watch the television series, "Mad Men" to get an idea of what it was like then. There were no nine-to-five hours. We worked until the job was done to make printing deadlines. If I had to write a jingle for a toilet paper, it had to get done that night or you stayed 'til midnight.

That was a rough way to make a living then with the competition and harassment on a daily basis. It was ruled by men for sure. It taught me to be tough and get a thicker skin. I learned never to settle and to stay in integrity.

It taught me that many of the men in the advertising world had a lot to learn about how to treat women with respect. No longer can men make harassing statements with sexual overtones on a constant basis and get away with it, or demote you because you refused to date or sleep with your boss. I remember having to do a lot of work in the one advertising firm's darkroom where they created all the film work for our ads.

One day I was wearing a sweater with a picture of a bicycle on the front and the men in the darkroom asked if they could ride my bike and all started laughing like it was hysterical because my boss thought it was funny. Really? They couldn't get a date if they paid for one. We've come a long way, baby, since then but we have a long way to go. We're survivors for sure. It made me stronger and that's where I lost my timid little girl side, growing up in the corporate fast-track lane of advertising. I had to learn to stand up to these idiots or get walked on.

Real quick, I grew a back bone, took the knowledge they gave me, created my own publishing company in 1980 and co-published a hardbound book, "Ohio, You Have Something to Crow About!" all while still working full time for the ad agency. The vice president didn't find out until days before our book signing at the biggest downtown bookstore because it was advertised in the largest Ohio newspaper. He almost choked on his coffee reading it. Ha! Take that, you turkeys. Keep staying in the darkroom. Maybe one day you'll see the light.

So, do we ever really graduate from Earth School? Hmm, not really because we *never* stop learning, even on the other side. Every life is a nano-blink. Earth School is a place you come to grow in all ways and filter out the B.S. If you don't learn your lessons the first time, you just get them again in another form. They may be with different actors or actresses but there's no hiding from them. A lesson will keep coming back to you until you figure it out. Pay attention if the same scenarios keep repeating and you can't figure out why.

For some of you, you keep ending up with the same type of spouse over and over again. Many marriages later, you continue to gravitate to the same type of person and can't figure out why your heart is still so unhappy. It's probably because you are seeking happiness outside of yourself. We're trained very early on that if we just find our magical prince, he'll kiss us and we'll get on his white stallion and trot off into the sunset where he'll take care of your every need. Newsflash, this is not a Disney flick and the bluebird of happiness is not going to swoop down to sew your clothes for you.

**LESSON:**

*Learn to be more independent. I've seen more women become bag ladies because once they leave their husbands or vice versa, they soon find out they have no skills. After being married for a long time, they raised children who pulled them away from their talent as being the best stenographer in the world, a job that is no longer needed. Heads up! No one is hiring a typist with carbon paper anymore. And, if you're lucky enough to own your own business, hiring a millennial will be a real shock to you. They won't start work before 10 am and want more money per hour than a top executive. They only know Snapchat and Instagram and think Facebook is for old people.*

*Bottom line, to truly grow, you have to get through all your life lessons first and the only way to do that is to experience them. If you haven't learned by now, the key is humor to getting through those frickin lessons. Good luck! The biggest speed bump I see in clients' growth is that they take things personally and when that happens, they beat a negative scenario to death. We've all done it. We're human.*

*If you forgot how to laugh at yourself, again good luck. The more aggravated at life you get, the more life will hand you a bigger pile of lessons. Trust me, save yourself a whole lot of time and just find the humor in as much as you can. Nothing is worth getting strung out over. What many don't understand is that the Universe just may have something bigger in store for you that you can't see from where you're sitting, spouting about what a wreck your life is. All the Universe can say is "wish granted." So again, for the umpteenth time, watch your thoughts and words that come out of your mouth. If I had a recorder taped to you, you'd probably be shocked at the things you say on a daily basis that you aren't even aware of.*

**"All the world's a stage and all the men and women merely players: They have their exits and entrances; and one man in his time plays many parts, his acts being seven ages."**

William Shakespeare

## AFFIRMATIONS FOR CHAPTER 3

I am wise enough to understand that I am enough and that it is not acceptable to be harassed or abused by anyone!

I enjoy my sense of humor and know that it carries me through many crazy times.

I find the blessing in all things.

I understand that when doors close, that there are more doors opening elsewhere.

I see obstacles as new opportunities for growth.

*Joanne unveiling a painting*
*to*
*600 people at Yellowstone National Park.*

# CHAPTER 4

**DAMMIT, NOT AGAIN!**

Wow, what was I just talking about in Chapter 3? So, here it is, a big lesson for myself as this literally just happened on November 8, 2018. Anyone who has read my first book, "Surviving Earth School," knows that my one fear is driving on freeways after almost getting killed in 1980 when a drunk driver hit my husband and me and totaled our car.

We were in Phoenix at a global, well-known spiritual conference with many best-selling authors. I was a vendor there with my visionary art and we drove from Chicago to get there with all my art that is just too bulky to ship. I was a bundle of nerves being the passenger the whole way as I watched other drivers weave in and out of traffic across the country while texting and not keeping their eyes on the road. People are so oblivious. We drove three days through New Mexico, Texas and Oklahoma in areas where I thought I'd lose my mind as there's nothing to see for hundreds of miles. On top of that was the stench of cow manure and fertilizer thrown in for good measure.

The show itself was fine and I made some great contacts. One gal in particular, Paula from Ireland was such an incredible soul that when we met, we both felt like we knew each other from another lifetime. The connection was that strong. She bought my book and connected with it and then as luck would have it, or "divine timing" as I call it, my husband and I ran into her in a restaurant that was at a different place from where our show was and invited her to sit with us. Our waiter had literally seated us within a foot from her. We discussed how we could possibly create a seminar in Ireland as nothing like this was available there and people were slowly awakening, wanting more knowledge to enlighten them. If it's meant to be, it will unfold.

When the conference was over, we said our goodbyes to those we met. Paula came down to the vendor area and told me again how moved she was by my book. Saying goodbye to her was like saying goodbye to a long-lost sister.

The whole time we were packing up, all I could think of was, "Oh God, now we have that long-ass drive back to Chicago." If I could have changed my mind, I would have paid someone to drive our van back and just hopped a plane. It's the most tedious, boring drive you can imagine and thank God, my earth angel husband, John, or "Saint John" as I call him, drove. My son, Bob, was smart and flew home. I remember asking one of the vendors there, Frankie to pray for us as we headed home. I just didn't have good vibes about the drive home.

We made it through Arizona, New Mexico, Oklahoma, Texas and Missouri with no rain or traffic jams. We were only one hour from home just south of Joliet, Illinois, in a little town called Channahon. We were on I-55 north in the left lane and out of nowhere this huge, orange double decker car hauler, loaded with cars, decided to change lanes and come into our lane without even looking.

John laid on the horn and swerved over into the grass to hug the guard rail and of course, the one who is the most paranoid about being in cars on the damn freeway, me, is closest to this monstrous hauler veering towards us. All I remember is recoiling and waiting for the impact as this wall of orange metal filled with cars moved into our lane colliding with us on the passenger side and ripping off sheet metal the length of our van. The sound of it will stay with me forever. Metal flying and all I thought was, "Shit! Not AGAIN!!" as I recoiled thinking that if I pulled myself in, even an inch, it might save me.

If John hadn't swerved into the small patch of grass when he did, I'd be flattened right now. After the outside metal was ripped off, the top of the passenger door window was so twisted that the window was splayed out about eight inches at the top and sides. Cold air turned this wreckage into a refrigerator within seconds adding insult to injury. Thank God it wasn't pouring or snowing. The snow arrived the next day.

At that point, I did a check list in my head. "Ok, I'm still alive, my husband is alive, I can't see the damage because there's no side mirror anymore, I can't see what things look like out there and it must be bad if there's that much open space at the top of my door and all around it. I can't open my door. Will the car explode next? Are we sticking out in the left fast lane where we might get hit again? Why isn't anyone stopping? They're all flying by us as if we're invisible.

The toughest part of life are the lessons we experience here in Earth School. They can seem brutal at times and we draw to us that which we fear.  What do *you* fear?

Interesting, all I could think to do was grab my cell phone and post that we just got wiped out on the interstate. I was still shaking.  Instantly, messages started coming in from all my friends telling me to breathe and not to panic. Reading so many kind words truly helped my mind settle down.   I felt the love through their endearing messages. I can't even explain it.  I could feel their prayers coming to us like rays of light.

Yes, I knew angels or some higher power had to have come between me and that moving wall of metal but I could see visible messages coming in lighting up my phone constantly giving me hope and courage.  Reading so many positive words to breathe and not to panic, kept my strength up.  Come on Joanne, you're a warrior, a survivor. You can get through this! So, for all of you who messaged me in that moment, there are no words that can express my gratitude.  Thank you! It was like having you all there to support me. I didn't realize how much I was loved.

To top things off, John had to have a four-hour surgery two days later and had eight long metal screws placed in his one foot. He needed six months to heal that. Again, trying to find humor in this was no easy feat but I did manage to draw a woman's face on the foot of his cast. The doctors and nurses at the hospital got a kick out of it.  He was an easy target as he slept from the pain killers.  Hey, they couldn't expect me to sit at his bedside nonstop overnight twiddling my thumbs.

*Shhh! He'll never know!*


It was only a week before our accident that a friend of mine showed me a picture of her nephew's car in the same situation where a semi came over in his lane and flattened his car into the guard rail. Miraculously, he crawled out of the back window even though nothing was left of the car. At least the trucker that hit him stopped. The driver of the car hauler that hit us kept going, as did everyone else around us. Not one person stopped. Not one person thought to get the truck's license plate number and call it into the police. What the *hell*?!

I can't even begin to tell you how terrifying it is to be trapped in steel. I couldn't move as the divider console was to my left, a twisted door on my right and no way to get out. I was in shock and wondered who from behind might hit us next. What's with people today that not one person stopped or called the highway police? As someone mentioned to me just the other day, people are suffering and have their own problems.

No one wants to get involved if it doesn't affect them directly. Did this trucker know he even hit us? How could he not have? Once again, I felt so damn violated and then the *what if's* crept in. That's the worst. *What if* this happened on that ungodly stretch of nothingness in Oklahoma and we were left alone on the side of the road? *What if* we were crushed? *What if* we had died? The mind never stops when you're in shock.

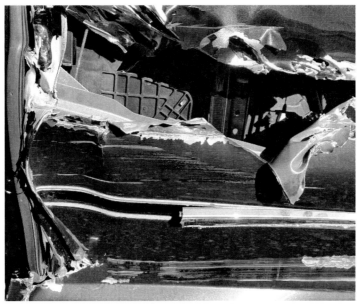

**The Aftermath**

**LESSON:**

Through that whole scenario of the hit and run accident, I can tell you that LOVE is truly all there is. How many times have we read that in spiritual self-help books but took it with a grain of salt? In my time of need as I was trapped on the side of this highway, the one thing I really felt coming through was the LOVE of my friends messaging me that they were praying for us or that they loved us or to be strong or that angels were protecting us, that God had our backs, but the LOVE is what came through all of those words.

That love is what kept me afloat until we could get home. I could feel the sincerity of every heart-felt message. It doesn't cost a thing and yet we don't tell our friends and family often enough just how much they mean to us and how much we truly love them. I want you to know right now *how much you are loved and how much I appreciate you. I've never been so grateful in my entire life to get another chance here in Earth School. As crazy as that sounds, I love doing my work here to help humanity. It certainly isn't an easy place to live as you will go through your ups and downs and experience your highest and lowest ebbs.*

*When it comes to life lessons, you'll be stretched further than you ever thought possible and when you think you can't handle one more thing, a thousand other things hit you. Somehow, with enough determination, you make it through. We are amazing beings. We truly are. I'm actually blown away to think of some of the mind-boggling events I've been through. Looking back now, I honestly don't think I could handle those situations again.*

*I hate the word "tested" but boy, there are times I really feel like we are pushed to our mental and physical capacity with only one weak string left on that life line and it's about to snap. Just when it seems the last thread of that rope is about to pop, you're reeled back in.*

*The one good thing about all of these lessons is that when you complete them, think of the knowledge and especially the wisdom you acquire. When you graduate from Earth School, all the wisdom you gained goes with you. You keep that. It's like you have this gigantic library stored in your etheric self that just keeps growing. That is how I can tell when someone is an old soul. It is how they handle difficult situations.*

*The wise master who's been around many lifetimes seems to find the blessings and humor in what most would totally freak out over or harbor hate and anger over.*

*They're in it for the long run and don't give up the first time things don't go their way. Marriages or any relationships are work. They require investments. They're like a rare flower that constantly needs tending to. So many are not willing to put the time into a relationship as it is a work of art when you think about it. The more you hone and polish it, the greater the masterpiece.*

What does it mean, to be dead?  Not that I was at that moment.  When you die, there's actually an increase of energy meaning you vibrate higher than when you do here on Earth.  Some describe it as changing the frequency on your old-fashioned radios.  You just keep dialing away until the right station comes in clearer.  You go through some changes in many ways. Frequency for one, the rate at which you vibrate is increased.  Remember, we're here in this dense energy.  All you do is shift over to another bandwidth or vibration to where you fit comfortably.  Death is a grand shift in your consciousness. You simply ascend to another dimension.

**"Those you meet and interact with are either reflections of a repeated cycle or lessons you need to learn from or to teach them something.**

**Pay attention to the difference."**

*Joanne Koenig-Macko*

## AFFIRMATIONS FOR CHAPTER 4

I am beyond grateful for being so protected at all times.

I am thankful for my guardian angels who watch over me.

I know that everything happens for a reason and that it puts things into perspective as to how lucky I am to still be of service here.

I am grateful for my husband and partner who supports me in all that I do.

I am thankful for a new car that is safer than the one before.

I am beyond grateful for so many friends that are there in times when I need them the most.

I understand the power of prayer and love.

I am grateful to meet new friends around the world.

*Plant seeds of kindness daily*

## TEN MISTAKES TO AVOID

Remorse over yesterday's failures.

Anxiety over today's problems.

Worry over tomorrow's uncertainty.

Waste of the moment's opportunity.

Procrastination with one's present duty.

Resentment of another's success.

Criticism of a neighbor's imperfections.

Impatience with youth's immaturity.

Skepticism of our nation's future.

Unbelief in God's providence.

*Anonymous*

*"Crystal Cave" by Joanne Koenig-Macko*

*"Flying Fairies" by Joanne Koenig-Macko*

"It was then that he began to drift with the wind like a leaf blown from a tree. And he was not able to distinguish whether he was riding the wind or if the wind was riding him."

*Lieh Tzu*

## POSITIVE CHANGES IN THOSE WHO EXPERIENCED A NEAR DEATH OR BRUSH WITH DEATH

Most live their life with purpose

Most want to help humanity in some way.

Most rediscover what life is about.

Most do not get upset over the little things in life.

Most have an altered viewpoint and are happier.

Most notice a marked difference in their appearance.

Most realize that love is all there is.

Most are more honest with themselves and others.

Most realize a change in moral values and religious views.

Most have a stronger relationship with spirituality.

Most seem to mellow out and are more balanced.

Most will avoid getting caught up in others' dramas.

Most are quick to forgive.

Most are more appreciative of everything.

Most relish friends and family more.

Most are more connected to nature and its beauty.

Most have a new lightness and fun about them.

Most realize that heaven and hell are here and now.

# CHAPTER 5

## HOW TO MASTER OPENING HEARTS

Just recently, I finished the last show for the year, 2018. It was a small elementary school bazaar, a much different vibe than I was used to but I knew that this wasn't about how much art I could sell, rather spending quality time with my grandchildren, daughter-in-law and son who were there. That was the school my granddaughter, Luci,  attended. It was a great way to support her school as well.

I was still rattled emotionally and physically from the hit and run accident I had just experienced a week prior. The trauma was still fresh and my feelings were raw. My joy was lost and part of me really wanted to stay home where I didn't have to think about anything in the outside world. I really needed a cave at that point. My trust in humanity was shot, I was tired from the busy show in Phoenix, the drive across the U.S. was too much and I just got through a scary hospital experience with my husband who had a serious foot reconstruction surgery.

Needless to say, my mind just wasn't set on selling anything or dealing with the public. Thank God I went to this school fair. What I witnessed was far greater than anything I can remember in a long time. My granddaughter, Luci, who was four years old at the time helped me at my table, bagging my books. She instinctively knew to start handing out little gold foil angels to people that came to our table. They're very small, something you would slip into your pocket or wallet. I love sprinkling them inside my books when I mail them out. I watched this amazing child come out of her shell and eventually leave our table to go up to total strangers in wheelchairs, the elderly or just about anyone in need of a smile and hand them one of these gold angels to watch over them.

When you're at a booth all day, you get to observe everyone around you and most people are so sad or look lost. The world's a crazy place right now. There's so much going on in our government, the politics, the fires in California, endless shootings. You can see it weighing on people, let alone, what's going on in their personal lives. How many are struggling with illnesses, or relationship problems or monetary problems, especially during the Christmas holidays.

And here is Luci going up to each of them with this amazing smile on her face and gifting them with these little gold angel sprinkles. Luci truly came from her heart. Working with her that day was like getting hit over the head with a valentine. I watched the innocence of this little earth angel and how she touched the hearts of these people, one at a time. It was magical and it was being witnessed by so many in this big room that day. I watched the people's faces go from sad to joyful as Luci made them smile again. By the end of the day, the entire mood of the show had shifted. People were laughing again.

She also had this great idea after all the angels were handed out, to take a legal pad around the show and asked people to write their first name and then to draw a flower next to their name. Between the angels she gifted and the names written down, she touched at least 100 people that day. When we packed up and were leaving the building, people would stop me and say, "Boy, I sure hope she never loses that joy!" Or they'd stop her and say, "There's Luci, my new best friend!"

She filled me and so many attendees with such love and joy that day to the point where I had no time to think about the accident or my husband's recent surgery that week. I had something new to remember, how a small child, in total glee, turned hearts on and *truly* made a difference. She gave people hope. She showed them how to smile again and that their input mattered. What a gift and it didn't cost a cent. Little did she realize how much she helped heal her Grandma Macko that day.

If you want to elevate your game, all it takes is doing kind acts. Let people know you truly care and that they matter. Do it unconditionally, expecting nothing in return. People are lonely. Many are scared, many are hurting emotionally, physically, mentally and some are spiritually broken. They may have lost their faith in God or in humanity. It can be a pretty cold world out there as many are so focused on their own problems that they don't have time to love one another. One small act of kindness can turn someone's life around and may prevent another from taking their life that day. Everyone wants to be loved. Everyone deserves to be loved. To receive love, you must first give it.

What can you do to help another that doesn't cost anything? I know this sounds silly but the other day, I bought a carton of eggs and the next morning when I opened it, stamped on the inside of the lid, it read, "Good Morning, Beautiful!"   What a cool idea for that egg company to do.   They just brightened someone's day.   It sure as heck brightened mine!

*Luci's Names Collected at the Show*

51

LESSON:

*The most important lesson for this chapter is that you really don't have to spend any money to make a difference in another person's life.*

*All it takes is a kind word or thoughtful deed to make someone feel special. We've all received unexpected gifts in the past. Make sure you give back to keep the blessings coming. Things don't necessarily come in the way of finances. Gifts come in many packages and the best ones are unexpected.*

*When you give, make sure you are not expecting something in return or it is not "unconditional love." The ego will tell you, it's all about you and that someone must reciprocate. You never know if you've come here to earth school to work out karma with another individual. Follow your heart. It's the best compass and it won't lead you astray.*

**"A simple act of kindness can transform and lift another's soul. You'll never know how much you affect another when you make them feel included and that their input is important."**

*Joanne Koenig-Macko*

**AFFIRMATIONS FOR CHAPTER 5**

I am beyond grateful for my children and grandchildren who constantly teach me what matters this lifetime.

I know how and when to be a powerful influence on those around me.

I know that a kind word or a thoughtful deed can make a tremendous difference in another's life and I know when to act on that guidance.

I understand it doesn't cost a penny to lift another's vibration so that they feel that they matter in life.

# CHAPTER 6

MESSAGES FROM MAMA

So many wondrous things are unfolding. I recently had an incredible public reading in front of an audience by a celebrity medium from California, who called me out by name from an audience of over 300 attendees. He told me there were over 100 deceased people in a group all wanting to talk to me  and that my mom, the "Rose connection", led the pack! Ha!

Just like my mom, being the Leo always wanting to be heard, front and center. According to the medium, they referred to themselves as "Team Joanne" and my mom was the head spokesperson with my dad, Frank, there as well. My grandfather, Anton, along with many others, including my dear friend, Cheryl who transitioned years ago, joined the entourage.

The medium told me I must have been a "very good girl" because these people were all telling him that I helped so many of them. He even mentioned how my grandfather walked me to a corner beer garden in the fifties to buy me an orange soda for a nickel and knew it was Fanta soda! That was our very special date. These are special moments I'll never forget. This was the most incredibly accurate reading I've ever had.

Interestingly, at the same event that evening, I met several beautiful souls who just so happened to be sitting in front of me in the audience. When I had mentioned to the medium that I had just published a book, the women in front of me asked if they could purchase it and we struck up a conversation which resulted in them visiting me at my home. The one gal, Alicja, moved to the U.S. from Poland at age 17 and truly has an incredible gift as a clairvoyant. I find from talking to so many incredibly gifted mediums, that they've gone through a lot of pain or transformation. It's almost like a rite of passage. I can't explain it.

Alicja and I talked for hours and she shared how a neighbor who recently passed, showed up in her bedroom and how it frightened her. When her deceased neighbor showed up again the next night, she took Alicja's hand and led her to her neighbor's grieving daughter who was still crying over her mom's passing. Alicja watched as her neighbor kissed her daughter's forehead to comfort her.

For some, the gift is just more prominent from an early age. If you don't understand it, it can be alarming. We all have the gift. It's just that some have more clarity and it starts earlier in life. Some are afraid of it and shut it down immediately. No right or wrong.

As an empath and coach, I regularly give messages to others to help them in life. That's why I love what I do so much because it's helping humanity in so many ways. It reminds them how powerful they truly are. It's like giving a client a new pair of glasses.

The detail that the medium from California gave me was over the top 100% accurate and indeed gave me confirmation of my path writing books. They conveyed that my books were the key to teaching overseas. So, if anyone reading this has connections to Europe or the U.S., let's see where this all goes! I love speaking to large groups. I've already been asked to speak in Italy and Ireland. Let's plant the seeds and watch them grow.

Telepathy has always fascinated me. What does it take to communicate with the deceased and why do some do it with such clarity, easy and grace? They say we all have the gift, it's just that some practice it 24/7. This medium that read for me got his practice by being a taxi driver in California. He always had an audience in his back seat and got lots of clients as a result of it. Practice is key! Just like any craft, the more you do anything, the better you are at it.

I remember working on clients when I was in my sweet spot or what I referred to as being in the zone. The messages would come in very clearly, especially if I worked on an empty stomach. Probably because food has energy and can be heavy when you are tapping into the other side. You certainly don't want to eat steak and potatoes before a reading. Remember, everything has a vibration. Certain foods will lower your vibes. Coffee for one is very grounding and that would be my last choice to take prior to a session. Water with fresh lemon or a drop of lemon or grapefruit essential oil works best for me. Again, check with your doctor as grapefruit may not mix with certain medications. What works for me may not work for you.

Another supplement I find that helps with mental clarity is raw B-12 methyl cobalamin vitamin. Raw simply means the ingredients were never heated. I take 1,000 mcg but always check with your doctor first. *Make sure it's the methylated version.* It helps fire the neurons in the brain and lifts your mood. It helps with many things but the mental clarity for readings is key. The ancient Greeks taught that the herb, rosemary, was great for remembrance and is another good one to use. I just don't care for the smell or taste of it. I find it too pungent for me and I don't care to smell like a leg of lamb.

The brain and muscles send out pulsing electrons which are, in fact, your radio program for the human body. Much of the phenomena of clairvoyance, telepathy and psychometry can easily be understood by reference to the science of radio and electronics. To talk to the other side, you're just picking up their frequency. In order to do that, you must get in a place where it's quiet so that you have no other radio frequencies interfering. It's key to have a quiet place or have relaxing non-verbal music.

I highly recommend my son, Bob Macko's music for this purpose. His album, "Aelysium" is my favorite and trains you to breathe with the music so that you get the optimal amount of oxygen deep into your lungs. Most of us are shallow breathers. Again, we are receivers and the most important receiver is our brain. We must protect it and keep it from agitation or frustration. Those are frequency squashers for sure!

Whenever we think, we create electricity. When you're calm after meditating, you'll have a smoother frequency without all the crazy peaks and crashes that excessive voltages can generate by being angry or alarmed. Inner composure is key and that's why it's a great idea to find a quiet place without interruption or noise when you desire to connect with a departed one.

The average person has way too much to worry about these days. Obsessing over debt, jobs and the news, disrupts your frequency. Learn to breathe deeply and slowly. When you do shallow breathing or pant heavily, you just rob the brain of oxygen. Breathing deeply is key to emptying the lungs of stale air, probably stored since Christmas morning of your sixth birthday, lol. No, seriously, learn to breathe deeply and slowly. Practice, practice, practice! The quieter you can get your brain, the better the messages. Have fun!

*Bob Macko in Sedona*

**LESSON:**

*A good clairvoyant knows the importance of deep breathing, plenty of oxygen and finding a quiet place to empty your head so that you can hear the messages.*

*If you are getting negative messages to go out and do harm to anyone, you are not getting messages from a higher source. Common sense, guys. I had a client who swore that Archangel Gabriel told her to sell off all her furniture, move to Las Vegas and work in the casinos to "flick" energy to the gamblers.*

*I couldn't convince her otherwise and she ended up spending her life savings playing Keno while attempting to clear casinos of bad energy. All she accomplished was clearing out her bank account of a million dollars and becoming homeless. A little common sense goes a long way.*

**"Your intuition is a birthright. Everyone is born with their own unique way of tapping into source. Use it wisely. I pray the children of today do not forget that they have this precious gift as they rely so much on technology. Families have even lost the art of a good conversation over dinner."**

*Joanne Koenig-Macko*

**AFFIRMATIONS FOR CHAPTER 6**

I know that when loved ones transition, they are still very close and work with me in precious ways.

I know the difference between good energy and bad by the message being given to me.

I know how to be a good listener.

I know how to be compassionate and when to offer my services for those in need.

I understand that people must make their own choices for their own growth.  Allow them their journey.

I understand that our deceased friends and relatives are never really gone.  They are here to help us and it's ok to acknowledge them.

## Cardinal sign

*I was truly moved by my deceased family members coming through so clearly at the event I recently attended. Some say that when you see a cardinal, it is a deceased loved one letting you know they are near you and helping you.*

*Interestingly, as I was writing this book, a bright red cardinal would land on our patio railing and perch itself outside my office window. If I took a day off from writing, it wouldn't be there. Makes you wonder how loved ones who have crossed over try to get our attention.*

*Some say a cardinal is illustrative of a departed loved one and one of the signs of heaven. When you come across one, it might mean they are stopping by. They mostly appear when you miss them or need them the most. They may also visit for the duration of celebration as well as sadness to watch over you and to ensure that you know they are with you always.*

*Cardinals are frequently believed to be spirit signs from heaven, mainly because of their bright red color. When a cardinal shows up at the instant a departed loved one is being talked of or thought of; it could most likely be your loved one trying to make you feel that they are right there with you. They are associated with the number 12. I kept hearing to do 12 chapters for this book and got confirmation when I found out that cardinals are associated with that number!*

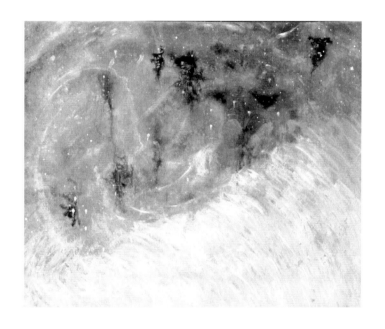

*"The Gathering" By Joanne Koenig-Macko*

## HOME

"When I'm gone, please, do not grieve.

For I am Home and you will see

that signs abound from up above

to show you all there is, is LOVE.

Bless Your Heart, stay young at heart,

Fear not for we did not depart.

Forever I'll be by your side so just enjoy

this wondrous ride."

*Joanne Koenig-Macko*

# CHAPTER 7

## GOOD VIBRATIONS

Everything in the universe vibrates! Everything. I remember visiting the Rock and Roll Hall of Fame in Cleveland, Ohio, many years ago and something stayed with me from that visit. The museum had a Beach Boys display with interviews on videos that the public could watch. This one video I happened to catch was about how one of the Beach Boys wrote the song, "Good Vibrations." It's about picking up vibrations between love-struck girls and boys in their teens. Here's what prompted that song.

Brian Wilson's mom told him how dogs can pick up on your vibrations and that they can sense if you're afraid of them or not. He received this lesson as they were out walking and a stray dog approached them. Interestingly, that song was part of their *Pet Sounds* project. Fear has a vibration, joy has a vibration, *everything* has a vibration so what are you putting out there to the world? Let's look at this further.

Most of you are aware of the musical scale: Do Re, Mi, Fa, So, La, Ti. These tones or vibrations were once used in ancient Gregorian Chants before the "Do" changed from UT and before Si was added and later changed to Ti. These tones were believed to give tremendous spiritual blessings when sung in harmony during the old religious masses. So, how did those notes even come to be? They date back to almost one thousand years ago. What is now called "Do" used to be "Ut." Its original term was "Ut Quent Laxis."

The note, "**Re**" came from the term "**Re**sonare fibris" meaning to *reson*ate, expand, amplify in this particular Hymn to St. John dating back to the 700's. "**Mi**" came from the term "**Mi**ra gestorum" which basically translates to wonderful or **MIRA**culous deeds, "**Fa**" came from "**Fa**muli tuorum" translated to "We, Your" which is about connecting and relationships.

These six notes (now seven) were the first syllables of words in a song or hymn to Ioannem or Saint John the Baptist to remind us that *we are servants here to do God's work and by singing these vibrations, we are basically clearing our lips and minds of any negativity or guilt so we can do wonderful deeds and heal ourselves as well via vibration!*

Some say those notes or tones were altered by the church so the healing did not take place, therefore removing our powers that be and giving them up to the church. Interesting. If you want to hear something hauntingly beautiful, just look up a Gregorian Chant on the internet, "Medieval Gregorian Chant, Invitatorium: Deum Verum" by Etienne de Liege. The sounds and vibrations were healing and resonated in the hallowed halls that were created so that sound could carry and reverberate through your entire being back in the day.

We know that when sand is sprinkled on a vibrating surface, it forms unique patterns, depending on the frequency. The higher the pitch of sound, the more intense and intricate the patterns become. This was discovered by Ernst Chladni and the term "cymatics" would come to be as a result of his research.

Interestingly, researchers discovered these strange symbols carved in cement stone blocks in the Rosslyn Chapel and realized that it must have been a musician who carved these in the ceiling of this ancient church. It turns out those symbols were actually cymatic symbols, each depicting a note and when the code was deciphered, it played a song. The ancient masters knew the power of healing with tone and vibration. We simply forgot as so much research has been destroyed. Some say that the heavy stones of the Great Pyramids were actually moved using high-frequency sound. Just look up research on the Hutchinson Project to see how certain frequencies can elevate objects.

What does this all break down to so that the ordinary person on the street makes any sense of it? When you are in the feeling of utter joy, you vibrate a certain frequency. Every organ in your body at that point is singing as well or vibrating. It's in that state of rapture where healing occurs. It's hard for "dis"ease" to exist. When we lower our frequencies to that of fear or anger, what do you think is happening to the cells of your body? We can raise those frequencies through the help of instruments, singing and sound but to keep it as simple as I can here, stay in a state of joy, ease and grace. That is quite healing in itself!

It's no wonder those who stay in constant states of depression or anger and blame everything and everyone around them for their misfortunes are more prone to illness. I truly believe that is why cancer is so prevalent now.

Stay in gratitude! Eat high-vibrational foods, use high-vibrational oils, surround yourself with high-vibrational art and watch what comes out of your mouth 24-7. Associate with high-vibrational, positive people and cut out the gloom and doom that's weighing you down.

### FREQUENCIES FOR SOUND HEALING:

**Blood – E, 321.9 Hz**

**Adrenals, Thyroid – B, 492.8 Hz.**

**Kidneys – Eb, 319.88 Hz.**

**Liver – Eb, 317.83 Hz.**

**Intestines – C#, 281 Hz.**

**Lungs – A, 220 Hz.**

**Colon – F, 175 Hz.**

**Gall Bladder – E, 164.3 Hz.**

**Pancreas – C#, 117.3 Hz.**

**Stomach – A, 110 Hz.**

**Brain – Eb, 315.8 Hz.**

**Fat Cells – C#, 295.8 Hz.**

**Muscles – E, 324 Hz.**

**Bone – Ab, 418.3 Hz.**

I have a feeling that as we continually raise our frequencies, these notes and tones will also be altered as well. We've advanced quite a bit since Medieval days. I have to admit, there are days watching the news, I often wonder if we're not regressing when I see some of the hatred out there amongst certain groups.

Speaking of frequency, have you followed the activity of the Schumann Resonance? It went absolutely crazy on March 15, 2019.  So, what is the Schumann Resonance?

It's the frequency of the Earth or vibrations she radiates that can be measured scientifically from her surface up to the ionosphere. There are global electromagnetic resonances generated and excited by lightening discharges in the cavity formed by the earth's surface and ionosphere. Call it an "atmospheric heartbeat" if you will. Scientists have also noticed certain cycles that are picked up and measured when certain events happen globally that impact humanity as a whole.

Earth is indeed a living, breathing entity so we really need to take care of her more and stop poisoning her and blowing things up, let alone using force to extract oils from her which displaces her mantles, causing more earthquakes as plates become unstable....just common sense, folks. This fracking nonsense is creating chaos. The Schumann Resonance is normally around 7.83 to 9 Hz and on March 15, 2019, it shot up to 150 Hz!

Those who are truly sensitive, felt it in different ways.  I got so dizzy that weekend that I couldn't walk a straight line and no, I wasn't drinking.  It got so bad; I asked my husband to take me to the emergency room where I was checked out thoroughly.  They did a brain scan with contrast dye and couldn't find anything wrong.

It subsided after five hours but let me tell you that was pretty scary! I even went to an ENT (ear, nose, throat) specialist to make sure no inner ear infection was present and after more testing, he found nothing wrong either.

After talking to several "sensitives" that weekend, I found out people had the same experience, along with pressure in the head and feeling like they were in someone else's body.

The bill was $28,144 for a 5-hour hospital visit, not even an overnight stay, to find out everything was normal. Thank God for insurance! Better to be safe than sorry.


LESSON:
*You are the only one responsible for your actions. Do what you can to raise your frequency. If we are all connected, we can change the planet for the better. If we all focus on the healing of our beautiful earth, we can create heaven on earth.*

*Everything vibrates. If you continually lower your frequency with bad thoughts or words, it can affect your health! Be mindful.*


**"The link between man and nature can never be broken. Mother Earth is a precious, living entity and we must treat her with the utmost respect for all she has given us."**

*Joanne Koenig-Macko*

## AFFIRMATIONS FOR CHAPTER 7

My vibration continually rises as I work on myself.

I know how to be responsible for my actions.

I know that the *feelings of positivity I* put out to the world attract that same frequency to me in whatever I do.

I know how to respect Mother Earth at all times and to treat her as a living entity that she is.

I know how to listen to my own body as to what nutrition or healing modality it needs at any given time so that I can enjoy optimal health.

## ONCE YOU GO HOME...

I've talked to countless people who have died, crossed over and came back.

The one thing they all share is that Love is all there is. There is no judgement, no anger or hatred in that new vibration. Many have commented on the flowers there. They each give off a tone or note so that a garden would become an actual symphony of sounds. Everything is communicated via thought, not word.

Dogs, cats, pets or any animal with red blood has a soul and gets to go home as well. Many loved ones' pets await them as they go Home. Many are greeted by relatives, friends who were very near and dear to them.

Some are immersed in an incredible light which is all sensory. Some are told it's not their time, that they still have work to do here in Earth School. That would be the hardest once you get a taste of Heaven or this incredible place of just overwhelming love.

Thoughts are instant. There is no sickness or disease and yes, you do get a life review. If you were a bully or hurt anyone here physically, you'll get to see that and how it affected the one you hurt.

Just a reminder, live life to the fullest while you're here before you graduate so you're not repeating lessons over and over. Life is precious and is over in a nano blink. Make it count!

# CHAPTER 8

## WELCOME TO THE SHIFT!

Have you noticed the chaos many are in now? Friends, neighbors and relatives may be going through a lot now but the world in general is going through growing pains. The old ways are crumbling. Third world ideas and actions cannot exist as larger groups of enlightened people start standing in their power. As I  type this, the churches are experiencing more changes and holding special councils to address their old problems that in the past, were swept under the carpet. Some Cardinals are being defrocked. More priests are being arrested, globally. This is affecting many who look up to their church for hope and comfort. My friends in Ireland and Australia are telling me it's even worse there as far as the problem with the priests who were evicted because of their actions.

Beyond the churches, look at what is happening in our government now. It's total chaos on the Hill. I'm amazed they can get anything done as they bump heads and clash constantly, pitting one against the other. Venezuela is in total upheaval over who should lead their country. North Korea keeps testing missiles when they promised not to and the President just sent 1,000 troops to the Middle East. No wonder people are on edge. It will be interesting to see how it all plays out.

As I type this, the news is now breaking that at least 50 high-powered people, some in Hollywood, are going to be in big trouble for paying off key people to get their kids higher test scores in college. Here we go folks! Not like I didn't see this coming in the age of transparency.

Get your popcorn out and pull up a theatre chair. It's going to get really, really interesting! The Shift is on.

LESSON:
*Everything is transparent now. Stay in integrity or you'll be flushed out. With the new, higher vibrations, you're going to see huge shifts and changes in the world. The corrupt will fall but not before a great fight.*

*It's like the dark is fighting the light now. Stay in balance and harmony. Take care of YOU. Don't sit in front of the television set all day. It'll drive you nuts. Besides, most of it is all negative, sensational news anyway. Work on perfecting you.*

**"Keep your thoughts positive because your thoughts become your words. Keep your words positive because your words become your behavior. Keep your behavior positive because your behavior becomes your habits. Keep your habits positive because your habits become your values. Keep your values positive because your values become your destiny."**

*Mahatma Gandhi*

**AFFIRMATIONS FOR CHAPTER 8**

I know how to be positive in all things I say, do and create.

I know that the vibrations of positivity make a difference.

I am grateful for the transparency that is happening on a global basis in order for great change to take place.

I fully understand that in order for great change to take place that everything starts with my words and actions.

# CHAPTER 9

## INTEGRITY

Funny, I was just discussing with my sister, Joyce, how the world is not the same as it was growing up in the fifties. Back then, there were values. Families watched everybody's children in our neighborhood.

Where did the breakdown begin? Kids in large cities are randomly shooting passersby in cars as part of initiations into gangs with no remorse. That's how badly they want to belong or be part of another group. The same is happening to the decaying neighborhood I grew up in as a kid in Cleveland, Ohio, where people just randomly break into homes and have no problem stripping a home of all its copper piping to sell it for scrap.

As my mom used to tell me when I was a kid, "Life isn't always fair, honey." It's facing those traumas and trials in life, those unfair shakes and growing from them. If life knocks you on your butt, learn to get up just one more time. Do one more thing from that experience that empowers you instead of crying victim. What a loser calls defeat, a winner calls a learning experience. Defeatists enjoy telling their tales of woe over and over to anyone who'll listen while a winner will look at that scenario and use it to teach from, move forward and grow.

All we can do is continually work on ourselves. The more we work on us, the better off we'll all be. There's always room for improvement to be a better person, to take the high road instead of looking for vengeance. Do not hold onto anger. It's not worth it! But do learn to stand in your power by making people accountable if they have wronged you. Big, big difference between getting even and holding someone accountable. As Buddha said so eloquently, "You will not be punished for your anger, you will be punished *by* your anger."

As you continually work on yourself, your light will become brighter. The brighter your light is, it's like the moth to the flame. More people will be attracted to it. Never think bad thoughts or wish ill on anyone who has wronged you. So, suck it up, buttercup and keep moving forward. This too shall pass.

### LESSON:

*Life doesn't always turn out the way you think it will. When you feel the world is dumping on you, the best way out of that poor me situation is to turn around as quickly as possible and be more compassionate to other people. Help another in need. Most importantly, help another with no expectation of getting something in return.*

*If you are upset because they don't return the favor, then it wasn't given in love unconditionally. And, if you're a true friend, you won't allow your friends to swim in that pity pool. Hold your friends to a higher standard. In that way you are empowering not only them but yourself by walking the talk and setting the example as the way shower.*

"A negative attitude toward others will never bring me success. You are searching for the magic key that will unlock the door to the source of power; and yet you have the key in your own hands, and you may make use of it the moment you learn to control your thoughts."

*Napoleon Hill*

## AFFIRMATIONS FOR CHAPTER 9

I know how to be a good friend to others.

I know how to be reliable.

I know how to trust my instincts.

I know that I have the key to unlock any door in life.

I know when to use the above affirmations for the highest and best good of all.

*"Through the Gate" By Joanne Koenig-Macko*

# CHAPTER 10

**MOVES LIKE JAGGER!**

One thing's for sure, no one knows when your time is up. No one knows when it's your time to elevate from Earth School. We may be shocked when that moment arrives and we may not be ready for it. This is why time is so important. If you have any grand dreams,  make them come true before you wake up on your sofa and realize that you're 92 years old and did absolutely nothing but complain about how life short changed you. In reality, it was you who short changed yourself by not ever taking action, even if you failed at it.

Think about what you really desire. Do you have a bucket list? What would make your heart sing? When you find your passion, you'll move mountains because you'll be doing what you want and not what you think you should be doing because it was expected of you. When that fire's in your belly, you'll find a way to make it happen.

I remember when I drove to a major hotel, signed a huge contract for ballroom rental, food and filling 100 rooms to the tune of $20,000+ and God knows what else I had to cover outside of hotel expenses without a dime in my pocket. I never thought that people may not show up. That thought wasn't on my radar. Once I signed that contract, there was no other place to go but get busy and make it work. I was going to prove to myself that I could make this happen. That was 21 years ago and I'm still running my Lightworkers Conference. If I had listened to everyone who said I was nuts, I would have never challenged myself to make it happen. You must first believe in yourself. Every entrepreneur takes chances. It's how you break through to the next level.

As I look back now, things that people told me would be impossible to achieve, I did and am still. I've traveled the world many times over, sailed to amazing remote islands, married a wonderful man and still with him for 40 years, have two amazing sons, beautiful daughters-in-law who gave me three incredible grandchildren. I've run successful seminars for 21 years and touched countless lives to remind people that they can do whatever they dream! My art reached the world just as I knew it was going to when I saw the vision at age five.

It's through my writing that I realize how much I've accomplished in 70 short years. God willing, I'll live 'till I'm 100+. But only Creator knows when my time's up here in in this dimension. I just hope my body can keep up with my 30-year-old attitude! Lol.

It sucks when your mind says you've got the moves like Jagger but your body says, "Oh, *hell* no, you don't!" Or, you can remember what you ate for lunch in kindergarten but you can't remember where the heck you put your glasses or that they're on your head as you search frantically for them. Hey, if that's my biggest problem, I won't lose sleep over it. As my mom used to say, "Old age is not for sissys."

So, nurture yourself. And, dance like no one's watching! When you stop moving, you're screwed and tattooed. Just watch Mick Jagger still running around the stage like a chicken without its head. He's iconic and damn, he's still doing the prostate shuffle while his drummer gums his Lorna Dunes. Gotta give 'em credit.

Love that our old-time rock bands we grew up with are still pushing it! They still have the big ol' hair, gold chains and leather pants. Ok, news flash, some of you really need to retire already before you dislocate a hip up there. Read my lips: You can no longer do the splits on stage! The only one who still performs effortlessly is ZZ Top. All they have to do is stand still on stage and spin their guitars around. They still have it. Oh yeah. They can be 120 years old and still do that. They don't move for a reason. They're not wearing out any body parts. They're safe. They'll make it.

There's nothing you can't do if you put yourself to the task. That means taking action, not praying or meditating by your mailbox daily waiting for checks to simply drop from the sky. Most people get excited about new ventures but then when they realize it's going to take an action plan; they freak out and make excuses why they shouldn't move forward. Were you ever stuck in a one-horse town and realized you were going nowhere? As the late Jim Rohn used to say, "If you don't like where you are, MOOOVE! YOU'RE NOT A TREEEE!"

The most successful people are willing to do what 97% of the others won't. They're willing to take risks and they don't focus on the failures of some of those risks. They're too busy moving forward because they took what they've learned from the setbacks and ran with them.

Everything you do in life here is to make you grow, including the failures and the rewards.

Don't settle. Don't just be here to survive. You want to thrive! And that means doing something that makes your soul sing, whatever that is to you. I remember interviewing a doctor many years ago who was known nationally for his field of expertise. He told me if he could do it all over again, he'd never be a doctor. When I asked him why, he shared that his dad was a doctor and his grandfather was a doctor so it was just expected of him to follow in their footsteps.

The rules kept changing over the years so he got paid less and less for procedures that in the past, he was paid a lot more for. His heart truly wasn't into it. How sad to think that his patients weren't getting the love from this man who they looked up to, especially for their well-being. So, there's another hint. Don't do what's expected of you just because everyone in your lineage was expected to carry on the family business. My grandfather was a shoe cobbler in Austria. I doubt that could pay the house mortgage today, -- well, unless he was a Louboutin.

**LESSON:**
*You are unstoppable. Never underestimate your strength. Your only fault was that you listened to the little demons in your head that kept telling you that you can't. Sucker punch that little fairy sitting on your shoulder who tells you that you won't make it or that you're not good enough, or that you'll fail miserably because you don't have the funds to follow your dreams. Some of the most successful companies in the world started out in a garage in*

*someone's home.  Most inventions were created because of a mistake trying to create something else.*

**"If you're constantly afraid of taking chances, then be ready to grow moss at your feet.  Everything takes courage. Thinking outside the box is a start. Doing something differently and better will get you to the next level of growth.  The adventure will be educational either way."**

*Joanne Koenig-Macko*

## AFFIRMATIONS FOR CHAPTER 10

I know how to live my life with passion and to dance like no one's watching!

I have the courage to take chances knowing that the Universe has my back, especially when helping humanity move forward.

I know how to create and implement a game plan in order for something major to be created.

I know how to overcome my fear of failure and live my life fully and to be present.

I know that showing warmth, compassion and respect for others will take me farther than technical knowledge and efficiency.

"Infinity" Photo by Joanne Koenig-Macko

List what you'd like to accomplish yet this life time.

1.

2.

3.

4.

5.

6.

7.

8.

9.

10.

11.

12.

13.

14.

15.

# CHAPTER 11

## YOUR COUNCIL ROCKS!

Even the angels are learning from us. They must be in total, utter amazement of what we go through here in Earth School. They bow to us because this is no easy gig as you know by now. Would you really want to skip any grades and miss certain lessons?

The students who study more go on to reach higher awakening. They've mastered more lessons by experiencing a myriad of situations. Not everyone wishes to work on their lessons and then wonder why they are still stuck attracting the same type of people, the same problems and the same scenarios over and over ad nauseum.

Before you get to Earth School, there are conferences on the other side. Your council or spirit advisors get together and based on how many lessons you need to learn and the depth of those lessons, you and your council choose your family with the best fit for your growth. In short, your council rocks!

Remember, it doesn't matter how many millions of dollars you earned while here. When you go home, none of that money or material things you accumulated go with you. What does go with you is the wisdom or knowledge you acquired.

Another awesome thing that happens when you graduate is that if you were in a toxic marriage or had horrible parents, you will not see them on the other side because in the spirit world there is the Law of Harmony which means anyone you meet there you will get along with wonderfully and peacefully. If you had very loving relationships with your parents here in this dimension, just know that you will be reunited with them on the other side. Those in harmony can be with each other in that higher vibration once they cross over or go home. Love is all there is when you go home. There is no room for ego, jealousy, hatred or any negative vibrations. It simply cannot exist there.

I can't emphasize enough that it is *crucial* that we work on ourselves here now so that we can in turn help others grow and awaken to their magical, wondrous selves and create heaven on earth.

## LESSON:

*At the end of each year, I always ask myself: "What did I do to make a difference in someone's life this past year? Did what I do this past year to make an imprint? Did it add to my legacy as a game changer? Did I do something to work on myself for more balance in my life?*

*If everyone took these steps, we certainly could create heaven on earth. Remember, heaven is a state of mind. You are your thoughts in action. Are your thoughts helping you go forward in life or keeping you stuck in fear and sadness? Only you can change that. You are that powerful.*

"**For everyone you meet, some will test you, some will use you, some will love you and some will teach you. But the ones who are truly important are the ones who bring out the best in you.  They are the rare and amazing people who remind you why it's worth it.**"

*Unknown*

**AFFIRMATIONS FOR CHAPTER 11**

I know how to master my life lessons with joy, ease and grace.

I understand that everything is on Divine Timing.

I know how to make every action count.

I know a great teacher when I meet one and I'm beyond grateful for the myriad of amazing teachers I've had this lifetime.

I am grateful for the legacy I am creating on so many levels.

*"Transformation" By Sofia Macko*

# CHAPTER 12

## THE LAWS AND MANIFESTING

One of the first things I learned from my global studies with masters and through first-hand experience is that there are countless laws of the Universe. The great masters taught this for centuries, long before it hit western civilization. There are  too many laws to cover or my book would be a foot thick. I'll focus on the ones I feel will help you the most. Let's have fun with this!

**LAW OF USE:** I guess the best way to teach this is through example. There was a lady who took much of her earnings and was obsessed with buying clothes. She had so many clothes in her closet that price tags were still on them for years. I actually knew a woman like this in California and when she gave me the tour of her closet, it was an Oh, my God, experience! She took me clothes shopping and snapped her fingers as a buyer followed her throughout the store. She would point to what she wanted and order one of every color. Her closet was jammed with clothes she never wore. She was a compulsive spender.

It was crazy. I knew the Law of Use would kick in sooner or later. Sure enough, within the same year, she lost it all which I won't get into. What you don't use, you lose. You can't hoard guys. She was bringing in so much for her selfish, egotistical reasons, it had to blow up in her face and it did.  If you're not using something for a long time and it's creating clutter, get rid of it, sell it or donate it.  It becomes stagnant energy that helps no one except the dust bunny and the moths.

**LAW OF SYNCHRONICITY**:  Have you ever been somewhere and a certain person was put in your path for a reason? I've had so many synchronistic moments, it's hard to remember them all.  I remember being at an outdoor show selling my art and a lady came to my booth to buy an art piece.  She handed me her credit card and on the card was the name, Joanne Macko.  Are you serious?  Ironically, her sister worked with my husband at the corporation he was with when we lived in Connecticut.  She knew she needed to be at that show and was looking for the perfect art piece. The Law of Synchronicity will put people in places where they need to be for a reason.

Just like the man who was in an online chat room one day in the nineties listening to my chat about how I painted an eight-foot angel. He ended up sending me $4,000 overnight to pay for that piece to be converted to lithographs by Christmas of that year.  Divine timing and the Law of Synchronicity work very close in hand.

**LAW OF ATTRACTION:** It's amazing to see how the Universe works to bring like vibration to match yours in specific instances.  If you are a high-vibrational person, do you honestly think you're going to be associating with thieves and ex-cons?  I doubt it.  You are attracted to like-minded people who think like you, have the same interests and are here to make a difference.  You are your thoughts and words in action.  As Jesus said, "The Kingdom is within you." He never said it was outside of you. He was saying that you have everything within you. You don't need to search for it. We radiate a frequency. That energy is like a magnet that attracts the same vibration, no right or wrong about it. If something keeps annoying the hell out of you, what do you think you'll keep attracting in order to learn from that lesson? I once knew a college student who constantly complained about the police. He was a pizza delivery boy and wouldn't you know it, every time he turned a corner, he got a ticket when everyone around him was surpassing the speed limit and doing all kinds of crazy things yet it seemed he had this invisible sign on his car, to ticket only him. What he detested he brought to him to learn from.

**LAW OF POLARITY:** According to this law, everything has duality. Everything can be separated into two wholly opposite parts and each of those parts still contains the potentiality of the other. We each have good and bad in us, dark and light. Which ones do we choose? A good example of this law is when someone breaks off a relationship with someone. The person left behind usually goes into their dark side and only focuses on their depression, sadness and abandonment. The dual side of this is focusing on the bright side. Wow, I'm really lucky that she broke up with me because she would have been a control freak or a spendaholic. Maybe she disliked kids and you wanted children. There is a polar opposite of everything that happens. Which do you choose? You can see the glass as half full or half empty. Choose wisely.

**LAW OF CAUSE AND EFFECT:** According to this law, for every cause, there is a definite effect. Your thoughts and actions create specific effects that manifest and create your life as you know it. Change your thoughts and your actions and manifest the life you desire. If you're mean to people, they will be mean to you. If you give love, you will get love back. If you help others, others will help you. If you steal from others, they will steal from you. If you respect others, they will respect you. If you want to change your life, you must change your thoughts and actions. Ralph Waldo Emerson said it best: "Man becomes what he thinks about all day long." And dating as far back as the 17th century, in the Epistle of the Galatians 6:7: "...whatsoever a man soweth, that shall he also reap."

**LAW OF ACTION:** We can't get around this one no matter how hard we try. I see countless individuals who practice meditation, speak kind words, share their awesome thoughts and yet when I asked them what they are actually doing to match those words with the physical work, I hear crickets. You need a massive action plan or getting off your duffs to make it happen.

**LAW OF GENDER:** Law of what? Yep, gender. No, I'm not telling you to change your sex, silly. This law says that everything has a masculine (yang) and a feminine (yin) principle. In order to be a Master, you must find the balance of these two qualities. These two aspects are the basis for all creation. If you are a brand-new soul here in Earth School, you're probably leaning toward one or the other. Again, this has nothing to do with sex. Feminine aspects would include being sensitive, merciful, forgiving, kind, nurturing where the male aspect would represent standing in your power, leadership, and taking action. The true Master knows how to be a balance of both.

I thought it would be a great to give you some manifestation techniques to practice daily by writing these down. It's much better to write them instead of speaking them. Buy a beautiful journal where you can keep your manifestation statements contained in one area. You don't have to spend a lot on a journal. Every bookstore carries them.

What are you wanting to manifest? Perhaps you are embarking on a new job or want to change fields but you're unsure of what to do. Intuition is key in manifesting. I love asking my guides for signs so that I know I'm on the right track. Here is an example:

"Creator, reveal to me the way. Let me know if there is anything for me to do." I'll then ask my guides or Creator for a sign, sometimes as many as three signs to know if I should do a certain deed. It's amazing how those signs pop up. They can be on the side of a truck on the highway or in a television commercial, etc.

To create income, you may want to try this one:

"Infinite Spirit, open the way for my immediate supply. Let all that's mine by Divine Right now reach me in a great avalanche of financial abundance so that my (blank) is now paid for."

Ask if there's anything you need to do in order to receive the abundance. Listen to your guidance and intuition. Maybe you need to help another in need first to receive (Law of Cause and Effect).

See what comes to your mind's eye. What images do you get? Who knows? You may see yourself going to a different event than what you planned. When the truck driver hit us, I really didn't want to do any shows for a long time and I had one booked the month after the accident. I didn't want to be there so I asked my guides if it was in my highest and best good to go and I heard a resounding YES! It was at that show that I received the best healing I could get by working with my amazing granddaughter.

To receive joy, you must first give others joy. It took a child to remind me of several very important laws. I'm grateful. When I got it, vendors also gifted me with small gifts. It's as if it were a classroom, not a Christmas fair. I was the student and the five-year-old was the teacher. God, I am so blessed. Why do we make our lives so complicated? We're the greatest entertainment for those watching us from afar. They must shake their heads a lot and throw their hands up in the air watching us silly humans operate the way we do down here.


LESSON:
*Don't hoard or buy things just to buy them. If you don't use it in five years, sell or donate it. Don't buy something for the sole purpose of being the collector.*

*Pay attention to synchronistic moments. There may be something there you need. You attract what you give out.*

*Focus on the bright side of things. Find the blessing in all things that most would see as bad. What you put out there is what you get back. Start doing more good deeds.*

*Writing your intentions and witnessing them in your mind is key to creating that reality. Be specific as to what you desire. Asking for more money may land you just two dollars. Asking for a car may get you a rust-bucket special on the bottom of the lake. Asking for a tall and handsome man may land you a cardboard cutout of your favorite basketball player. If you're not sure what you desire, just say "Hey Universe, just surprise me!" Have fun with it!*

*When paying bills, be grateful that you have a car to make a payment on or that you have heat to keep you warm when it's cold or that you have light. Write your checks in joy or if you pay online, bless the payments for the gifts you are paying for. Write in the margin of the check why you are grateful to pay for that service or item you just bought. Use your imagination, get creative.*

**"The first power that meets us at the threshold of the soul's domain is the power of imagination."**

*Dr. Franz Hartmann*

## AFFIRMATIONS FOR CHAPTER 12

I understand the laws of the universe and how they work.

I know how and when to practice the laws of the universe in order for my life to work at its optimal best.

I understand fully that the universe sometimes has a different plan for me that is so grand that I cannot see it from where I am standing at the time.

I know how to trust the universe and let go.


**Speaking of the Laws of Manifesting, several years ago, the company who did all my printing on canvas called to let me know they were ditching that specialized machine as I was the only artist using it. I panicked! That would wipe my business out, I thought. They had to put it up for auction nationally and I was in no position to pay what it was worth. They told me if it didn't sell at auction, they'd negotiate with me to buy it outright. I put it out to the universe that printing machine was mine! When it didn't sell, they called me and said, "Hey, you're doing good work with it, how about $100 and it's yours." What?!?! So, I paid $400 to have movers bring it to me and install it in my office. Don't ask. It takes up an entire wall but bottom line, I manifested that one within days. Thank you, Creator! More please!**

**"Buddha" by Corey Grau**

# BODHISATTVA PRAYER FOR HUMANITY

"May I be a guard for those who need protection,

A guide for those on the path,

A boat, a raft, a bridge for those who wish

to cross the flood.

May I be a lamp in the darkness,

A resting place for the weary,

A healing medicine for all who are sick,

A vase of plenty, a tree of miracles.

And for the boundless and multitudes of living beings,

May I bring sustenance and awakening,

Enduring like the earth and sky

Until all beings are freed from sorrow

And all are awakened."

*Anonymous*

**Keep Smiling!**

## COUNSELING SESSIONS:

So many ask about my counseling sessions.

I've created what I refer to as my own version of "Angel Therapy" sessions. This is where I connect with you, the client and intuitively check in, with your permission, to see what I can pick up. I scan the body to see what is out of balance physically, mentally, spiritually or emotionally, what I refer to as P.M.S.E. I can see where energies are being held or blocked in any part of the body.

For instance, if a person has been stifled for many years or told to "be seen and not heard" or is not able to voice his or her truth, then I see built up energy or blocks in the throat area. Over many years, this can create a block in the flow of energy and can result in chronic neck or throat problems, especially thyroid problems. Just think of how life was in the 1400's where no one was allowed to say what was on their mind. Sadly, how many third world countries are still stuck there?

When I work on a client, it's a combination of energy work, counseling, intuitive work, getting rid of old beliefs that may be hindering growth and giving messages from either the angels, guides or departed loved ones.

Sketches and drawings are all part of that session. Sometimes it looks like scribble depending on what angel or master is coming through. Other times it's almost like an awesome drawing of their guide or guides. No two sessions are alike. I also add numerology to the mix based on their birthday. Numerology can show many things such as your life path (what you're about this lifetime) and your personal year and what that entails.

TESTIMONIALS FROM PAST CLIENTS:

*"I never have felt so much energy going through me before. I felt a lot of heat when you were working on me. It was so hot while you were working on me, I almost told you to stop because I was burning up. I had always felt pain in my knee and for the first time after the session, I'm playing basketballl with no pain!"* - A

*"Oh Joannee! We have some WONDERFUL NEWS that will make your holidays! Results from last Friday's tests showed that all the tumors are GONE. Yes, GONE. Even the large main one on the right side of the chest. We are still going through stem-cell transplant and we can handle that! All the positive energy and support that has been around us made this all happen and you are a part of that happening! We love you Joannee!* - S&B

*"One day I was talking to Joanne in an angel chat room on the internet and she was telling me about her paintings. I could hardly pick up a cup of coffee because the pain was so bad in my hands. I asked Joanne to pray for me*

*and we talked on the phone.  When I was done, I went into the kitchen and was able to pick up a coffee pot with no trouble! I started to cry and have not had any pain in that hand since. I believe Joanne has helped countless people. Bless you Joanne and Your Angels. I will never forget that night." – J*

*"Joanne, Audriana appeared to be cured. The doctor thought it was miraculous.  She told me that she really loves the pictures you sent her."  - W*

*"The information we have gotten from you, the insight into who and why has added to our strength.  So on this snowy morning, I'm writing to tell you how very grateful I am that you are woven into my tapestry...you have helped me so much to find my strength..and my laughter again...I hope your heart can understand what I'm saying, because words just aren't big enough..so from heart to heart I say, again, THANK YOU. – L*

**Side note:** I certainly cannot take credit for these people's healings. I do believe that when faith is strong, that anything can happen. Jesus even told his people, "I did nothing to heal you. Your faith healed you." I've worked on over 6,000 clients and we've seen many things that simply cannot be explained. Some heal with incredible results that no doctors can explain; some do not heal and some have made their transition. Some have actually seen angels in my house as I was teaching. On another occasion, one of my son's friends stopped by to visit and as he was pulling out of the driveway, he almost crashed into our mailbox because he saw a figure in white standing in our bay window.

I have noticed that those clients with the greatest sense of humor are the quickest to heal, even those with cancer. Those who harbor anger and depression usually self-destruct with their disease. Laughter truly is the best medicine.

**There was a funeral procession in the hills of California. The brakes went out on the hearse and it crashed into a drugstore and rolled right past the pharmacy counter. The corpse sat up as he flew by and yelled, "Hey, do you have anything to stop this coffin?" Ok, dad, there you go. The joke you told me when I was a little kid that always cracked *you* up every time you told it, lol.**

*Session Sketch of Someone's Guide*

*by Joanne Koenig-Macko*

## AFFIRMATIONS:

### For Abundance -

I love what I create and I attract financial abundance to me to continue my work and to help others as well.

Money is an exchange of energy. Others see value in what I do so that I may live an abundant life.

I am grateful for every bill I pay knowing that I am paying for a service or item that is beneficial to me.

I love what I do and am richly rewarded for it in many ways.

I attract abundance, not only financial but in the beautiful souls I collaborate with.

I know how to attract the finances to get my work to the world to truly make a difference.

I know how to use my creativity to secure the finances needed to live a beautiful life.

## AFFIRMATIONS:

### For Confidence and Courage -

I know how to live my life with confidence and courage to get through life's obstacles and experiences with joy, ease and grace.

I understand that courage is what it takes to get me to the next level of my growth and that I am protected and guided to try new things always.

I have the confidence and courage to try new avenues in order to always meet new people on my life path who may show me a better way.

I have the ability to know that I am courageous and confident to let go of something or someone who does not see my fullest potential.

I know what it's like to attract the high-vibrational masters to me that I can learn from and collaborate with for the highest good of all on my blessed journey.

## AFFIRMATIONS:

For Forgiveness -

I realize that everyone who pushes my buttons is my greatest teacher and to forgive them is the greatest gift for my sanity and theirs.

I understand the power of forgiveness and how to find the right words to forgive another for the greatest outcome for all.

I am grateful for the correct use of words to use in forgiving another.

I realize that I have the courage to forgive so that it can shift my life for the better, not the bitter. I know I can find peace with a certain situation and that forgiveness is key to healing.

I know that any crack in a relationship happens for more light to come in. I forgive anyone by knowing that they were hurting in some way to do what they did in the first place.

I am wise enough to understand that when people lash out, they are hurting inside and that this gives me a great opportunity to practice more compassion.

## IN CLOSING...

The main reason for writing this book was not to write an autobiography. It was more of a memoir written to help others through the lessons I encountered. My stories were shared only to enlighten you so that you could find the lessons in them that may help you in some way. Perhaps what I've shared will help you so that you don't keep repeating the same lessons over again. We don't want to repeat grade school. If I made you smile or laugh, then it was worth it. Perhaps by reading this, it will help you to share your stories of angelic visits. The more we open up about it, the more enlightened we'll all be.

So many are simply afraid to share their stories for fear of being made fun of or attacked. Trust me, I've gone through the mill with non-believers thinking I'm crazy or making this up. It took a lot to share my experiences but I believe it's time. So many are going through a lot now and need assurance that it's OK if your loved ones who have crossed over are appearing to you or leaving you signs. I'm here to remind you that each of you has your own burdens, your own shortcomings and your own traps to correct. Work on your own issues first before judging others. I'm simply here to remind you that you are more powerful than stooping to condemn others.

With all the mediums who now have their own tv series, it has certainly helped to discuss the unexplained more than ever. What they are doing is a great service to those carrying grief. It's also a huge reminder to love the ones you're with. Don't wait until they are no longer here and grieve over some petty argument you had that amounted to nothing. Tell your friends and family *now* how much you love them and appreciate them. Life can change in a nanosecond. Don't hold grudges because of pride. Be a role model for others so they know that love is key. Love truly is all there is. Imagine if everyone got this.

Which reminds me, why the heck are there so many people claiming to be the reincarnation of someone famous? I can't tell you how many Mother Mary's I've met, Saint John the Baptists and God knows, who else. I told an audience one year that one of these days, I'm going to get them all together, lock them up in a ballroom and have them duke it out as to who the *real* reincarnation of Mother Mary is. That may be the only way to solve this dilemma. I even met a man who claimed to be Jesus. He tried walking on water and I had to save him from drowning.

All said and done, I believe in you! You're an amazing, beautiful soul who stood in line to be here. So, get off the floor, dust yourself off and jump into this wonderful playground we call LIFE! Remember, people will forget what you said, but they'll never forget how you made them *feel.*

Until then, live your life as if every day was your last. Take time to smell the roses, get off your cell phones and meet with someone in person so you can connect heart to heart with them. Don't let that be a lost art. Learn to hug more, heart to heart. Know that you matter and that you are loved beyond measure. Now go and make your life count! Your Life begins right NOW. *And yes, you always had the keys. See you in my next book...Love, xxx*

## ABOUT THE AUTHOR

**JOANNE KOENIG-MACKO** is an international fine artist, intuitive counselor, author, professional keynote speaker and conference producer. She first discovered her gifts at the age of five when she realized it was her destiny to be a world-famous artist and humanitarian.

As a healing facilitator, Joanne has worked with over 6,000 clients from around the world, helping them clear old beliefs and coaching them on how to create their optimal life.

Joanne was the first recipient in the world for the "Wheel of Co-Creation in the Arts Sector." This prestigious award was presented to her by best-selling author and philanthropist, the late Barbara Marx Hubbard, of California, at an inaugural event held in Chicago for Joanne's contributions to help humanity through the arts.

Joanne's art has been collected around the world by countless world leaders, ambassadors and art collectors. Her art was published by Hay House for bestselling authors' books, including Doreen Virtue's *Angel Therapy* card deck and her art has been sold in Japan for at least eight years. She has also presented her art at the United Nations and served as Director of International Angels for World Peace, a division under the World Citizen Diplomats.

Joanne currently runs her annual Lightworkers Conference in the suburbs of Chicago and has created conferences to move humanity forward for over 20 years.

Joanne is available for keynote presentations,
book signings and long-distance counseling.

**JOANNE'S CONTACT INFORMATION:**

**Art Website:** www.JoanneMacko.com

**Email:** joanne@joannemacko.com

**Book website:** www.SurvivingEarthSchool.com

Facebook: www.facebook.com/SurvivingEarthSchool

*Lightworkers Conference:*
www.LightworkersConference.com

**Web development & graphics by Bob Macko:**

www.Lux-Productions.com

**Notes:**

**Notes:**

**Notes:**

**Notes:**